ALUMINUM

A TRUE BOOK®

by

Salvatore Tocci

Children's Press®
A Division of Scholastic Inc.

New York Toronto London Auckland Sydney
Mexico City New Delhi Hong Kong
Danbury, Connecticut

These pellets are made of aluminum.

Reading Consultant
Julia McKenzie Munemo, MEd
New York, New York

Science Consultant
John A. Benner
Austin, Texas

The photo on the cover shows aluminum cans. The photo on the title page shows crates of aluminum cans at a recycling center.

The author and the publisher are not responsible for injuries or accidents that occur during or from any experiments. Experiments should be conducted in the presence of or with the help of an adult. Any instructions of the experiments that require the use of sharp, hot, or other unsafe items should be conducted by or with the help of an adult.

Library of Congress Cataloging-in-Publication Data

Tocci, Salvatore.
   Aluminum / by Salvatore Tocci.
     p. cm. — (A true book)
   Includes bibliographical references and index.
   ISBN 0-516-23692-X (lib. bdg.)   0-516-25568-1 (pbk.)
   1. Aluminum—Juvenile literature. I. Title. II. Series.
QD181.A4T548 2005
546′.673—dc22   2004013148

CHILDREN'S PRESS, and A TRUE BOOK™, and associated logos are trademarks and or registered trademarks of Scholastic Library Publishing. SCHOLASTIC and associated logos are trademarks and or registered trademarks of Scholastic Inc.
1 2 3 4 5 6 7 8 9 10 R 14 13 12 11 10 09 08 07 06 05

Contents

Charles Hall developed a process to obtain pure aluminum in a woodshed behind his family's home.

What Did You Hear?

Do you remember the last time you heard something that you thought about for a long time afterward? In 1884, Charles Hall heard something he kept thinking about for more than two years. One day in chemistry class, Hall heard his professor say that the person who discovered an inexpensive way to obtain pure aluminum would become famous and rich.

In 1884, obtaining pure aluminum was very expensive. As a result, aluminum was valued even more highly than gold or silver. For example, the French emperor Napoleon III usually served his guests with dinnerware made of gold. For very special guests, however, Napoleon III served his guests with dinnerware made of aluminum.

After Hall heard what his professor said, he immediately started experimenting to find a cheaper way to obtain pure aluminum. In 1886, nearly two years after his first attempts, he finally succeeded. Hall's professor was right. Hall became

Hall left this chest to the company he founded. Inside are the tiny aluminum pellets he produced in his first successful experiment.

famous and founded a company that still produces pure aluminum today. He also became very rich.

What Is Aluminum?

Aluminum is an element. An **element** is the building block of matter. **Matter** is the stuff or material that makes up everything in the universe. This book, the chair you are sitting on, and even you are made of matter.

There are millions of different kinds of matter. However, there are just a few more than one hundred different elements. How can so many different kinds of matter be made up of so few elements? Think about the English language. Just twenty-six letters can be arranged to make up all the words in the English language. Likewise, the one hundred or so elements can

Aluminum is the third most abundant element in Earth's crust, or surface layer.

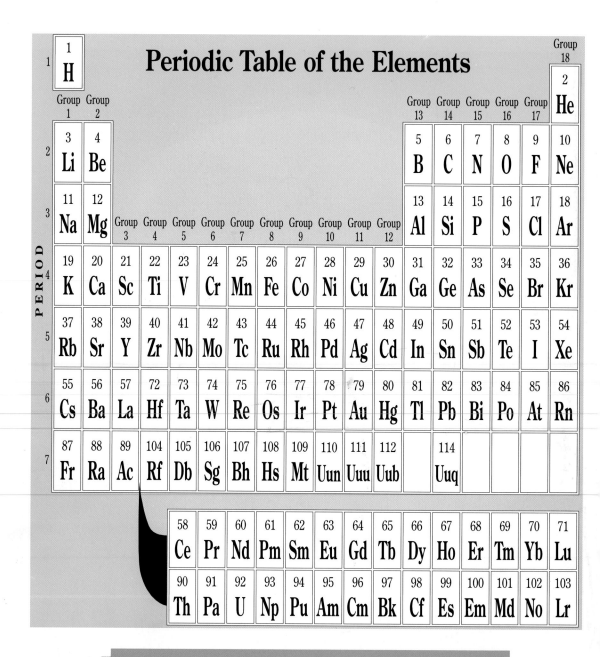

Periodic Table of the Elements

	Group 1	Group 2	Group 3	Group 4	Group 5	Group 6	Group 7	Group 8	Group 9	Group 10	Group 11	Group 12	Group 13	Group 14	Group 15	Group 16	Group 17	Group 18
1	1 **H**																	2 **He**
2	3 **Li**	4 **Be**											5 **B**	6 **C**	7 **N**	8 **O**	9 **F**	10 **Ne**
3	11 **Na**	12 **Mg**											13 **Al**	14 **Si**	15 **P**	16 **S**	17 **Cl**	18 **Ar**
4	19 **K**	20 **Ca**	21 **Sc**	22 **Ti**	23 **V**	24 **Cr**	25 **Mn**	26 **Fe**	27 **Co**	28 **Ni**	29 **Cu**	30 **Zn**	31 **Ga**	32 **Ge**	33 **As**	34 **Se**	35 **Br**	36 **Kr**
5	37 **Rb**	38 **Sr**	39 **Y**	40 **Zr**	41 **Nb**	42 **Mo**	43 **Tc**	44 **Ru**	45 **Rh**	46 **Pd**	47 **Ag**	48 **Cd**	49 **In**	50 **Sn**	51 **Sb**	52 **Te**	53 **I**	54 **Xe**
6	55 **Cs**	56 **Ba**	57 **La**	72 **Hf**	73 **Ta**	74 **W**	75 **Re**	76 **Os**	77 **Ir**	78 **Pt**	79 **Au**	80 **Hg**	81 **Tl**	82 **Pb**	83 **Bi**	84 **Po**	85 **At**	86 **Rn**
7	87 **Fr**	88 **Ra**	89 **Ac**	104 **Rf**	105 **Db**	106 **Sg**	107 **Bh**	108 **Hs**	109 **Mt**	110 **Uun**	111 **Uuu**	112 **Uub**		114 **Uuq**				

PERIOD

58 **Ce**	59 **Pr**	60 **Nd**	61 **Pm**	62 **Sm**	63 **Eu**	64 **Gd**	65 **Tb**	66 **Dy**	67 **Ho**	68 **Er**	69 **Tm**	70 **Yb**	71 **Lu**
90 **Th**	91 **Pa**	92 **U**	93 **Np**	94 **Pu**	95 **Am**	96 **Cm**	97 **Bk**	98 **Cf**	99 **Es**	100 **Em**	101 **Md**	102 **No**	103 **Lr**

A periodic table such as this one lists all the elements. Can you find aluminum on the periodic table?

be arranged to make up all the different kinds of matter in the universe.

Every element has a name and a symbol. The symbol for aluminum is Al, from the first two letters in its name. Like most other elements, aluminum is a metal. A metal is any substance that is a good **conductor** of electricity. Aluminum is the most abundant metal in Earth's crust.

Conducting Electricity

Fold a piece of aluminum foil several times to make a strip about 6 inches (15 centimeters) long and 0.5 inch (1 cm) wide. Tape one end of the foil strip to the negative end of a size C battery. Hold the metal base of a flashlight bulb against the positive end of the battery. Touch the free end of the foil strip to the metal ring above the base of the bulb. The bulb should light up. The battery produces electricity that flows through the aluminum foil and lights up the bulb.

There is more aluminum than any other metal on Earth. However, pure aluminum does not exist in nature, because aluminum will combine with almost anything it comes in contact with, including the oxygen in the air.

A substance that is made up of the combination of two or more elements is called a **compound**. A compound can be separated into the elements that make it up.

A powerful current of electricity and a very high temperature are needed to separate the aluminum from the oxygen in this piece of bauxite.

The compound that is commonly separated to obtain pure aluminum is **bauxite**. Bauxite is made up of just two elements, aluminum and oxygen. Separating these two elements was once a very difficult and expensive process. However, Hall developed a way to make it easier and cheaper to isolate the aluminum in bauxite.

How Is Aluminum Useful?

Hall was not the first person to isolate pure aluminum. The metal was first isolated by a German scientist in 1854, but the use of aluminum has a much longer history. About seven thousand years ago, the Persians made pots and

The ancient Egyptians used aluminum compounds to make cosmetics and dyes for their clothes.

bowls from clay that contained aluminum. About four thousand years ago, the Egyptians used aluminum compounds as cosmetics and as dye for fabric.

The world's first aluminum factory opened near Paris, France, in 1859. The French emperor Napoleon III provided the financial support to build it. Because it was worth more than gold, Napoleon III valued objects that were made from pure aluminum. The first object he ordered from the aluminum factory was a rattle for his only child.

Once Hall's process made aluminum much cheaper to produce, more factories were built to extract the metal from bauxite. As a result, people soon began buying objects made from aluminum. By the 1930s, aluminum kitchen utensils, coffee pots, and tea kettles were common household items. At that time, the company Hall founded stated that aluminum was being

Aluminum chairs became popular during the 1930s.

used for roughly two thousand different purposes, from constructing buildings to making statues.

Aluminum has many uses because of its properties. Aluminum is light but tough. It does not rust. It can be rolled into very thin sheets and shaped into different forms. Besides conducting electricity, aluminum also conducts heat.

Today, these properties have made aluminum foil a common household item that is used to store and cook foods. A more rigid aluminum foil is used to make pie plates and frozen food trays.

Aluminum has many uses outside the home as well. However, the aluminum is often first mixed with another metal to give it greater strength or a higher melting temperature. Mixing aluminum with another metal produces an **alloy**. Aluminum alloys are used to make planes, trains, and cars.

During World War I, an aluminum alloy became the metal of choice for making airplanes. Using this alloy to

Aluminum makes planes lighter
and therefore more fuel efficient.

build airplanes reduced their weight and cost. Today, aluminum alloys continue to be used to build both the bodies and engines of jet planes.

In 1935, the Union Pacific Railroad Company began operating the first streamlined train in the United States. Named the *City of Salina*, this train consisted of just three cars, including the engine, which were built from aluminum. This lightweight train could reach a speed of 100 miles per hour (160 km per hour). Today's high-speed trains can reach speeds of almost 190 miles per hour (300 km per hour). The bodies of these passenger cars are also built with aluminum.

In 1907, the Rolls-Royce Company was the first to build a car with an all-aluminum body. Today, aluminum is still used to make car bodies and engine parts. In fact, the body

This car can travel 70 miles (110 km) on 1 gallon (3.8 liters) of gas.

of the most efficient car in the United States is made entirely of aluminum.

The aluminum product that almost everyone comes in contact with is the beverage can. In 1965, a company started selling its soft drinks in aluminum cans. Today, aluminum is used to make more than 100 billion beverage cans each year in the United States alone. The use of so many cans has led millions of people to acquire a new habit—recycling.

Controlling the Flow

Hold an aluminum soda can in a sink. Use a small nail to poke a tiny hole in the side of the can, near the bottom. Notice that the soda pours out the opening, but then stops. The air surrounding the can pushes on the soda and stops its flow. Now poke another hole near the top of the can. The soda will again start to pour out of the bottom hole in the can. Air can now enter the can through the top hole and push down on the soda to force it out the bottom hole. What happens when you cover the top hole with your finger?

Why Should We Recycle Aluminum?

Even though Hall made it much cheaper to make pure aluminum, the process still takes time and energy. Three steps are involved. The first step is mining the bauxite. Dirt and other unwanted substances are always mixed in with the bauxite, so the second step is removing these substances. This part of the process involves grinding, washing, heating, and filtering the bauxite. The final product is a white powder.

The third step is melting the white powder. Normally, this powder melts at about 3,600° Fahrenheit (2,000° Celsius). Getting the temperature this high is a very expensive process. Hall developed a process in which the powder melts at about 1,800° F (1,000° C). Heating the powder to this temperature is much less expensive. A powerful electric current is then passed through the melted powder. Pure, liquid aluminum falls to the bottom of a container, where it is removed and cooled.

Aluminum, however, can be obtained in another way that takes much less energy than

The aluminum foil used to bake these caramel apples can be recycled.

getting it from bauxite—
recycling. Recycling aluminum
cans is easy. There are no

Used aluminum beverage cans are the most recycled item in the United States.

labels, caps, or tops that must be removed. Because the process is so easy, people in the United States recycle more than 60 percent of the aluminum cans they use each year.

Each year, roughly two million tons of aluminum are thrown in the garbage rather than being placed in a recycling container. Other aluminum items that are discarded include chairs, lawn furniture, window and screen frames, rain gutters, and kitchen appliances. To find out if something is made of aluminum, all you have to do is test it with a magnet. A magnet will stick to iron, steel, or tin, but not to aluminum. Anything that is made of aluminum can be recycled.

Recycling aluminum provides several benefits. First, it conserves natural resources. Between four and five tons of bauxite are processed to produce about one ton of pure aluminum. So, for every pound of aluminum that is recycled, four to five pounds of bauxite do not have to be mined from

Mining for bauxite involves tearing apart large chunks of Earth.

Earth. The less mining that is done, the more of Earth we preserve.

Second, recycling aluminum saves energy. It takes the same amount of energy to make twenty cans from recycled aluminum as it does to make one new can from bauxite. Before people started recycling aluminum, the aluminum industry used more electricity in one day than 100,000 people used in one year!

Third, aluminum does not decompose easily. Any cans or

other aluminum items that are tossed into a landfill will still be around in two hundred years or more. This is a long time, especially when you consider that the German scientist first isolated pure aluminum only about 150 years ago. Charles Hall's discovery of an inexpensive way to obtain pure aluminum has affected all our lives.

Fun Facts About Aluminum

- In 1807, a British scientist gave aluminum its name, even though he never could isolate it in its pure form. He actually called it aluminium, the name still used in England and elsewhere in the world.

- In 1852, 1 pound (0.37 kg) of aluminum cost $545. By 1897, the price had dropped to $0.37 per pound as a result of the process developed by Charles Hall.

- Recycling just one aluminum can saves enough energy to run your television set for three hours or to keep a 100-watt lightbulb burning for almost four hours.

- In 1884, a 6-pound (2.2-kg) block of aluminum in the shape of a pyramid was used as the cap for the Washington Monument.

- If placed end to end, the aluminum cans that have been recycled since 1972 could stretch to the moon and back 150 times.

- An aluminum can that is recycled today will be back on the shelf as part of a new can in about sixty days.

To Find Out More

If you would like to learn more about aluminum, check out these additional resources.

 **Books**

Farndon, John. **Aluminum.**
Benchmark Books, 2000.

Grist, Everett. **Collectible Aluminum.** Collector Books, 1993.

Llewellyn, Claire. **Metal.**
Franklin Watts, 2002.

Organizations and Online Sites

Alcoa
http://www.alcoa.com/ global/en/about_alcoa/ dirt.asp

Learn about the history of aluminum and how it is made at the Web site of the company Charles Hall founded. Read how a four-ton truckload of dirt is turned into a ton of aluminum.

Aluminum Association
http://www.aluminum.org

Click on "Recycling" to be taken to a list of articles dealing with this topic.

A History of the Aluminum Cap of the Washington Monument
http://www.tms.org/pubs/ journals/JOM/9511/ Binczewski-9511.html

This site provides an interesting story about the aluminum cap placed on the Washington Monument.

International Aluminum Institute
http://www.world-aluminum .org/history/index.html

Read about the history of aluminum, including the story of the French scientist Paul Louis Héroult, who simultaneously discovered the same process Hall did.

Use Aluminum to Clean Tarnish
http://www.creativekids athome.com/activities/ science_experiment1.shtml

Perform an experiemnt using a piece of aluminum foil to clean the tarnish off silver objects such as dinnerware and jewelry.

Important Words

alloy substance that is made by mixing two or more metals

bauxite substance mined from Earth that is the major source of aluminum

compound substance formed when two or more elements are joined

conductor substance through which electricity or heat passes

element building block of matter

matter stuff or material that makes up everything in the universe

Index

Meet the Author

Salvatore Tocci is a science writer who lives in East Hampton, New York, with his wife Patti. He was a high school biology and chemistry teacher for almost thirty years. His books include a high school chemistry textbook and an elementary school series that encourages students to perform experiments to learn about science. He and his wife make it a habit to recycle aluminum.

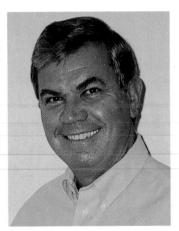